Dear Senior,

It's hard to believe this moment has come. We hope you have enjoyed looking back on the years and relationships and experiences that have brought you to this place. We hope you're looking forward to the years and relationships and experiences to come. You are not just at the end of high school but at the end of this season of adolescence.

The thought of being an adult may seem overwhelming but it is not all that bad. Hopefully you're looking forward to many of the responsibilities and freedoms that being an adult affords. You have people and resources to see you through the many obstacles, challenges, and leaps you'll take in your coming years.

But we, as the church of your youth, want to help in a particular way: we want you to continue your spiritual maturity. The Bible has much to say about what it means to be spiritually mature:

"The seed that fell among thorns stands for those who hear, but as they go on their way they are choked by life's worries, riches and pleasures, and they do not **mature**." (Luke 8:14, NIV)

"So Christ himself gave the apostles, the prophets, the evangelists, the pastors and teachers, to equip his people for works of service, so that the body of Christ may be built up until we all reach unity in the faith and in the knowledge of the Son of God and become **mature**, attaining to the whole measure of the fullness of Christ. Then we will no longer be infants, tossed back and forth by the waves, and blown here and there by every wind of teaching and by the cunning and craftiness of people in their deceitful scheming. Instead, speaking the truth in love, we will grow to become in every respect the **mature** body of him who is the head, that is, Christ." (Ephesians 4:11-15, NIV)

"But solid food is for the **mature**, who by constant use have trained themselves to distinguish good from evil." (Hebrews 5:14, NIV)

"Let perseverance finish its work so that you may be **mature** and complete, not lacking anything." (James 1:4, NIV)

Just as this is a new season of *life*, this is also a new season of *faith* in which you are called to maturity. And we want to help you do that. In this book, you will find 38 days of study that will help you know and believe God.

Dwell on those two words:
KNOW.
BELIEVE.
The two concepts go hand-in-hand. There are over twenty verses in the Bible in which the words appear together, revealing that knowing and believing work together. Here are just a few:

"'You are my witnesses,' declares the Lord, 'and my servant whom I have chosen, so that you may **know** and **believe** me and understand that I am he. Before me no god was formed, nor will there be one after me.'" (Isaiah 43:10, NIV)

"They said to the woman [at the well], 'We no longer **believe** just because of what you said; now we have heard for ourselves, and we **know** that this man really is the Savior of the world.'" (John 4:42, NIV)

"That is why I am suffering as I am. Yet this is no cause for shame, because I **know** whom I have **believed**, and am convinced that he is able to guard what I have entrusted to him until that day." (2 Timothy 1:12)

You can know God and believe Him only through His Word. And because of that, studying, understanding, and applying the Bible are the primary components to mature faith. Scripture study is

4

the key to a lasting walk with God. It's the key to continuing in the relationship you began with God in this church.

So we send you into your adulthood with this guide. It won't answer all your questions. It won't teach you everything you need to know about life and money and relationships and work. But it will show you how to **discover** God in His word so that you may **know** and **believe** Him. This Bible Study walks slowly through the entire book of First John. You'll learn the key terms, the history, the focus, and what the text meant not only for the first century church but for you as well. But more than these, you will know God more fully through this study, enabling you to believe Him more fully.

We are always here for your questions, your trials, your journeys, and your celebrations. Thank you for the part of your life story that included this church. We look forward to watching you mature in God as you know and believe Him.

Mike Miller, Senior Pastor
First Baptist Church Dickson, TN

**Instructions**

This is a straightforward Bible Study. However, there are a few things you'll need to complete it successfully:

Time. Every day, you'll need to set aside 15-20 minutes to complete the basic study. Don't skip anything! Each item in the study adds to your knowledge and understanding of the passage. There is an optional **Challenge** section at the end of each day that will allow you to dig deeper if you want.

Commitment. Don't start this—or any Bible Study—half-heartedly. Commit to completing it. The best way to commit is to set aside the same time every day, seven days a week. Give yourself some forgiveness and grace if you miss a day, but make it your goal to get in the seven-day-a-week habit of spending time with God in His word.

Honesty. You'll be asked to apply the passage to your own life, which will involve being honest with yourself and God. Don't back away from the challenge of holding yourself up to the light of God's Word.

Your Bible. Yes, each daily passage is printed (in HCSB translation) in the study. However, you may want to use your own Bible and make notes in it. You'll also need to look up other reference passages that are not printed in the study.

A quiet spot and a good pen. You are entering the presence with the Master of Creation through His love letter to you. Get rid of every distraction and prepare to hear His voice.
The pen is necessary; you may also want a variety of different colored pens, pencils, or highlighters if you're the color-coding type.

Some references for further study. If you can get your hands on a concordance or Word Study dictionary, that's great. But you might rather use blueletterbible.org (to find definitions of Greek word and do a complete word study) or biblegateway.com (for alternate translations). You won't need these references for the study itself, but we hope the passage inspires you to know more on your own. [All Greek words defined in this study are found at blueletterbible.org, Strong's Lexicon.]

<u>Creativity</u>. This study will give you many ways to look at God's Word, but it also gives you plenty of room to analyze and observe it on your own. The scriptures are double-spaced, providing you with plenty of room to color-code, underline, circle, or mark in a way that brings the meaning out to you.

<u>Prayer</u>. Start every study session with prayer. Praise God. Thank Him. Confess your sins. Lift up others. Focus on God and allow Him to speak clearly to you.

You can do this!

**Table of Contents**

### Day 1: Getting to Know John

This study takes a slow, intentional stroll through one letter, or epistle, of the New Testament: First John. We'll jump in feet-first tomorrow. But today, let's get to know the author.

The apostle John, who wrote this letter, was not only a witness to the life of Jesus Christ but also one of His apostles and one of the three apostles that got to witness things no one else did. He was also the author of the Gospel of John (right after Matthew, Mark and Luke) and wrote Second and Third John, as well.

Look up each of the following Scriptures about John's life at the time when Christ walked on earth.

**Matthew 4:18-25**
What happened?

What did John learn about Jesus?

**Matthew 17:1-13**
What happened?

What did John learn about Jesus?

**Mark 5:21-43**
What happened?

What did John learn about Jesus?

**Luke 22:7-13**
What happened?

What did John learn about Jesus?

**John 18:25-27** (John referred to himself as "the disciple whom He loved.")
What happened?

What did John learn about Jesus?

**Apply the Truth**: Recall one significant moment you had with Jesus. What did you learn about Him? How did He change you?

**Challenge**: In John's gospel, the book of John, he recorded his summary of Jesus at the beginning: John 1:1-18. Read it, underlining every description John made of Jesus.

10

**Day 2: 1 John 1:1-4**

**Read** this passage, at least twice, slowly. Out loud, if possible:

1 What was from the beginning, what we have heard, what we have seen with our eyes, what we have observed and have touched with our hands, concerning the Word of life—2 that life was revealed, and we have seen it and we testify and declare to you the eternal life that was with the Father and was revealed to us—3 what we have seen and heard we also declare to you, so that you may have fellowship along with us; and indeed our fellowship is with the Father and with His Son Jesus Christ. 4 We are writing these things so that our joy may be complete.

Circle the word <u>we</u> and <u>our</u> every time it appears in this passage.

Underline every phrase that describes <u>we</u>.

What do you learn about <u>we</u> in 1 John 1:1-4? (List at least 4 things.)

Who do you think <u>we</u> refers to?

Draw a square around the phrase "Word of life" in verse 1. Read John 1:1-5. According to John 1, who is the Word of life?

What other similarities do you see between John 1:1-5 and 1 John 1:1-4?

Find the phrase "so that" in verse 3 and verse 4. Draw a triangle around it. "So that" introduces a conclusion. What conclusion is listed after each "so that?"

Circle the main idea of this passage.

**Apply the Truth**: How have you heard or seen or observed Jesus recently?

**Challenge**: Look up John 15:11, the words of Jesus. Which verse in today's passage is similar?

**Day 3: 1 John 1:5-7**

**Read** this passage, at least twice, slowly. Out loud, if possible:

5 Now this is the message we have heard from Him and declare to you: God is light, and there is absolutely no darkness in Him. 6 If we say, "We have fellowship with Him," yet we walk in darkness, we are lying and are not practicing the truth. 7 But if we walk in the light as He Himself is in the light, we have fellowship with one another, and the blood of Jesus His Son cleanses us from all sin.

Review who you determined <u>we</u> to be yesterday. Circle <u>we</u> each time it appears in today's passage.

Review verses 3-4 from yesterday. Look at the word <u>Him</u> in verse 5. Who is <u>Him</u> referring to?

Verse 5 contains a strong, definitive statement of who God is. Write it in the space beneath the scripture in all caps.

The Greek word for light is *phos*, defined like this: "God is light because light has the extremely delicate, subtle, pure, brilliant quality; that which is exposed to the view of all, openly, publicly."

This same word appears four times in John 1:4-9. Write what you learn about the light in each verse:
Verse 4:

Verse 5:

Verse 7:

Verse 9:

According to 1 John 1:5-7, what must we do if we claim to have fellowship with Jesus?

**Apply the Truth**: Do you walk in the light? What areas of your life are in darkness?

**Challenge**: How many times did Paul use the word *phos* in his testimony in Acts 22:6-11?

14

**Day 4: 1 John 1:8-10**

**Read** this passage, at least twice, slowly. Out loud, if possible:

8 If we say, "We have no sin," we are deceiving ourselves, and the truth is not in us. 9 If we confess our sins, He is faithful and righteous to forgive us our sins and to cleanse us from all unrighteousness. 10 If we say, "We don't have any sin," we make Him a liar, and His word is not in us.

In yesterday's study, you examined the word *phos*, "light." According to verse 7, what two things happen when we walk in the light?

Verses 8 and 10 reveal four things that occur when we say "We have no sin." List them:

1.

2.

3.

4.

Several versions of Scripture (NLT, NCV, CEB, ERV) have the word Bu̲t̲ as the first word of verse 9. Write it in parenthesis as the first word in verse 9.

How does the word bu̲t̲ change the meaning of verses 8-9?

Who is H̲e̲ in verse 9?

What happens if we confess our sins?
"He is _____ and _____ to _____ us our sins and to _____ us from all unrighteousness."

**Apply the Truth**: Spend the next five minutes confessing sin. Ask God to reveal your sin to you. Agree with Him that **it is sin** and confess your need for forgiveness and cleansing.

**Challenge**: How many times does the word i̲f̲ appear in today's passage? Yesterday's passage? What is the significance of this little word?

**Day 5: 1 John 2: 1-2**

**Read** this passage, at least twice, slowly. Out loud, if possible:

1 My little children, I am writing you these things so that you may not sin. But if anyone does sin, we have an advocate with the Father—Jesus Christ the Righteous One. 2 He Himself is the propitiation for our sins, and not only for ours, but also for those of the whole world.

Briefly summarize the main idea of yesterday's passage:

How does 1 John 2:1 seem to conflict with the verse immediately before it, 1 John 1:10?

Write what you learn about sin in each of the following verses:

Luke 5:32

John 8:11

Romans 6:1-14

Is it possible to not sin?

Why, then, do we sin?

The Amplified Bible defines *propitiation* this way: "the atoning sacrifice that holds back the wrath of God that would otherwise be directed at us because of our sinful nature—our worldliness, our lifestyle."

**Apply the Truth**: In the space, write a prayer of praise to Jesus for taking away your sin and presenting you blameless to God.

**Challenge**: The Greek word for *advocate* is also used to describe the Spirit. See if you can find it in John 14:26.

18

### Day 6: 1 John 2:3-6

**Read** this passage, at least twice, slowly. Out loud, if possible:

3 This is how we are sure that we have come to know Him: by keeping His commands. 4 The one who says, "I have come to know Him," yet doesn't keep His commands, is a liar, and the truth is not in him. 5 But whoever keeps His word, truly in him the love of God is perfected. This is how we know we are in Him: 6 The one who says he remains in Him should walk just as He walked.

Read verse 3 and then verses 5b-6 (starting with the word "This"). Underline the phrase that is similar in both sentences.

What absolute truth does verse 3 reveal?

What absolute truth does verses 5-6 reveal in a similar manner?

The Greek word for <u>sure</u> in verse 3 and <u>know</u> in verse 5 are the same word, pronounced *gē-nō'-skō*, and means "to learn to know, come to know, get a knowledge of perceive, feel." Jesus used this word several times in John's gospel. Read them and note what Jesus says can be known:

John 5:42

John 6:69

John 8:32

What does verse 4 teach about someone who claims to know Jesus but doesn't live it?

**Apply the Truth**: Spend two full minutes reflecting on your obedience to God and daily walk. Do you know God?

**Challenge**: Consider verse 6. How did Jesus walk? Write 5 characteristics that marked His life.

### Day 7: 1 John 2:7-8

**Read** this passage, at least twice, slowly. Out loud, if possible:

7 Dear friends, I am not writing you a new command but an old command that you have had from the beginning. The old command is the message you have heard. 8 Yet I am writing you a new command, which is true in Him and in you, because the darkness is passing away and the true light is already shining.

The expression "Dear friends" is expressed "beloved" by many translations. In this letter, John wants to be sure that the recipients know they are LOVED.

Who loved them?

Who else loved them? (See 1 John 4:10)

The old command/new command described in this passage is the basis for this identity in being loved.

What does each of the following passages teach about love? (Note that Exodus and Deuteronomy were written by Moses around 1500 BC; John was written by John around 80 AD. These verses span the old and the new!)

Exodus 34:6

Deuteronomy 6:5

Deuteronomy 30:16

John 8:42

John 16:27

In the verses above,
How is love our identity?
How is love God's identity?
How are we commanded to love?

**Apply the Truth**: Does God love you? How do you know? Do you love God? How? Do you love others? How?

**Challenge**: Underline the words light and dark in this passage. Continue to search for these every time they appear in 1 John.

22

### Day 8: 1 John 2:9-11

**Read** this passage, at least twice, slowly. Out loud, if possible:

9 The one who says he is in the light but hates his brother is in the darkness until now. 10 The one who loves his brother remains in the light, and there is no cause for stumbling in him. 11 But the one who hates his brother is in the darkness, walks in the darkness, and doesn't know where he's going, because the darkness has blinded his eyes.

There are two sets of words that contrast each other in this passage. Circle them and draw a line connecting them.

According to verse 9, what is living in <u>darkness</u>?

According to verse 10, what is living in <u>light</u>?

According to verse 11, what happens when we walk in <u>darkness</u>?

Go back to 1 John 2:8 in yesterday's study. What does it teach about <u>light</u> and <u>darkness</u>?

Go back to 1 John 1:7 (Day 3). What does it teach about <u>light</u>?

Describe what it means to walk in the <u>light</u> based upon what 1 John has taught up to this point:

**Apply the Truth**: According to John 13:34, how should we love others?

Assess your ability to love by Jesus' definition.

**Challenge**: How many times does the word love appear in 1 John? Circle it every time you see it and make a list of all 1 John teaches about love.

### Day 9: 1 John 2:12-14

**Read** this passage, at least twice, slowly. Out loud, if possible:

12 I am writing to you, little children, because your sins have been forgiven because of Jesus' name. 13 I am writing to you, fathers, because you have come to know the One who is from the beginning. I am writing to you, young men, because you have had victory over the evil one. 14 I have written to you, children, because you have come to know the Father. I have written to you, fathers, because you have come to know the One who is from the beginning. I have written to you, young men, because you are strong, God's word remains in you, and you have had victory over the evil one.

Find the phrase "I am writing to you" and underline it each time it occurs. Find the phrase "I have written you" and underline it in a slightly different way.

For each phrase you underlined, circle the recipient.

Write the three recipients of John's writings:

What are the two reasons John chose to write to children? (See verse 12 and 14.)

What are the two reasons John chose to write to fathers? (See verse 13 and 14.)

What are the **four** reasons John chose to write to young men? (See verses 13 and 14.)

Do you think John meant the terms "children," "fathers," and "young men" literally? Who might they mean figuratively?

Into which category would you fall?

**Apply the Truth**: At different seasons of life, we have different challenges and strengths. Praise God for understanding your life right now, in the past, and in the future.

**Challenge**: Find John's approximate age when he wrote this. How might his age influence the people he called "children?"

**Day 10: 1 John 2:15-17**

**Read** this passage, at least twice, slowly. Out loud, if possible:

15 Do not love the world or the things that belong to the world. If anyone loves the world, love for the Father is not in him. 16 For everything that belongs to the world—the lust of the flesh, the lust of the eyes, and the pride in one's lifestyle—is not from the Father, but is from the world. 17 And the world with its lust is passing away, but the one who does God's will remains forever.

How many times does the word world appear in these three verses? Circle each of them.

What do you learn about the world from this passage? (Be specific.)

The word world is a Greek word pronounced *ko'-smos* (like the English word *cosmos*). It appears 58 times in the Gospel of John alone and 17 times in this book of First John.

Look up these verses and write what each teaches about the world:

John 1:10

John 3:16

John 9:5

John 13:1

John 14:27

Summarize the above verses: what are John's instructions to us concerning the world?

**Apply the Truth**: Write one way you struggle to separate yourself from the world. Confess that to Christ and ask Him to reveal His power to overcome the world.

**Challenge**: How does Titus 2:11-13 apply to today's passage?

28

### Day 11: 1 John 2:18-19

**Read** this passage, at least twice, slowly. Out loud, if possible:

18 Children, it is the last hour. And as you have heard,

"Antichrist is coming," even now many antichrists have come.

We know from this that it is the last hour. 19 They went out

from us, but they did not belong to us; for if they had belonged

to us, they would have remained with us. However, they went

out so that it might be made clear that none of them belongs to

us.

According to verse 18, where are we on the kingdom calendar?

Underline everything you observe about the Antichrist or antichrist in verses 18-19.

The Greek word for Antichrist (or antichrist; same Greek word) is any opponent of the Messiah.

John refers to the "last hour" twice in verse 18. That Greek phrase reminds us that in God's plan for all of humanity, we are in the final season: the season where people and things oppose Christ.

What are some prevailing thoughts or ideologies that oppose Christ in our world?

Circle the word remained (sometimes translated abided or stayed) in verse 19. This word also appears ten times in John 15:4-10. Read those verses and write what you learn about remaining/abiding/staying.

**Apply the Truth**: What are you doing to remain in Christ? What else should you do?

**Challenge**: You first studied the Greek word for "know" on Day 6. Review what you learned and apply that definition to verse 18.

### Day 12: 1 John 2:20-21

**Read** this passage, at least twice, slowly. Out loud, if possible:

20 But you have an anointing from the Holy One, and all of you have knowledge. 21 I have not written to you because you don't know the truth, but because you do know it, and because no lie comes from the truth.

Circle AND underline the word <u>But</u> in verse 20.

The words <u>but</u>, <u>however</u>, and <u>nevertheless</u> all introduce a **contrasting** idea in Scripture. Re-read yesterday's passage and keep reading straight through verse 20 to see the contrast. Summarize it here:

Verses 18-19:

**BUT**
Verse 20:

Note how many times the word <u>you</u> appears in today's passage. Underline each of them.

Who is <u>you</u>?

What do you learn about <u>you</u>?

Verse 21 asserts that John's readers know the truth. Summarize what John wrote about <u>truth</u> in Day 3, Day 4, and Day 6:

**Apply the Truth**: Do you know "the truth?" What is it?

**Challenge**: You'll be studying the word <u>anointing</u> more deeply on Day 15. Make a note to look back at verse 20 on that day.

### Day 13: 1 John 2:22-23

**Read** this passage, at least twice, slowly. Out loud, if possible:

22 Who is the liar, if not the one who denies that Jesus is the Messiah? This one is the antichrist: the one who denies the Father and the Son.23 No one who denies the Son can have the Father; he who confesses the Son has the Father as well.

John has already introduced the concept of the <u>antichrist</u> in this letter. Review the definition on Day 11 and what 1 John 2:18-19 teaches about antichrists.

According to verse 22, what else does an antichrist do?

This was a recurring theme among people who lived at the time of Jesus' earthly ministry: the unbelief that Jesus was God's Son. Read each of the following passages and write Jesus said about His relationship with the Father:

John 5:16-23

John 8:12-20

John 8:41-42

John 10:22-30

Using all you observed in these verses, answer the following: What is the truth about the Father and the Son?

**Apply the Truth**: How can you <u>confess</u> the Son and the Father (verse 23) today?

**Challenge**: How does John 14 more fully explain the Father and Son?

### Day 14: 1 John 2:24-25

**Read** this passage, at least twice, slowly. Out loud, if possible:

24 What you have heard from the beginning must remain in you. If what you have heard from the beginning remains in you, then you will remain in the Son and in the Father. 25 And this is the promise that He Himself made to us: eternal life.

This passage has several repeated words. Mark them in such a way that you can see them distinctly.

What **command** is given in the first part of verse 24?

What **conditional** (if/then) statement is given in verse 24?

Review what you learned about remain on Day 11. Summarize it:

According to verse 24, what must we do to remain in God and Jesus?

How does John 15:7 bring insight into today's passage?

What else do we learn about God's Word remaining in us in John 15:7?

Verses 24 and 25 are connected by the word and. This combines the truth of the two verses. What additional truth is revealed in verse 25?

**Apply the Truth**: What does the "promise" of eternal life mean?

**Challenge**: What similarities can you find between today's passage and the passage from Day 1?

**Day 15: 1 John 2:26-27**

**Read** this passage, at least twice, slowly. Out loud, if possible:

26 I have written these things to you about those who are trying

to deceive you. 27 The anointing you received from Him

remains in you, and you don't need anyone to teach you.

Instead, His anointing teaches you about all things and is true

and is not a lie; just as He has taught you, remain in Him.

According to verse 26, why is John writing the letter you are studying?


Consider what other verses teach about false teachers. Summarize each passage:

2 Peter 2:1-3


Romans 16:17


Matthew 7:15-20


The passages above were written by Peter, Paul, and Jesus, respectively. Each saw the danger of false or deceitful teachers.

According to verse 27, what is one key to not being deceived by false teachers?



The Greek word for <u>anointing</u>, pronounced *khrē'-smä*, refers to anything equipped by the Holy Spirit. It is the same Greek word used in 1 John 2:20 (Day 12). What does the anointing of the Holy Spirit teach you?


**Apply the Truth**: Read John 14:26: We must first know God's Word for the Spirit to teach us and remind us of it!


**Challenge**: Learn more about what the Holy Spirit gives through His anointing in John 16:5-15.

### Day 16: 1 John 2:28-29

**Read** this passage, at least twice, slowly. Out loud, if possible:

28 So now, little children, remain in Him, so that when He

appears we may have boldness and not be ashamed before Him

at His coming. 29 If you know that He is righteous, you know

this as well: Everyone who does what is right has been born of

Him.

Which words or phrases in today's passage have you seen in previous passages from 1 John?

Underline the phrase, "So now" in verse 28. This phrase (as well as "therefore," "for," "so that," "for this reason," and others like them) are terms of **conclusion** or **summary**, meaning a defining statement is being made. What conclusion follows the "So now" in verse 28?

Most Bible scholars believe John wrote this book near the very end of his life, when he was at least 80 years old. Who, then, would he consider to be "little children?"

Reflect on verse 28. Why might we be ashamed at Christ's coming?

How does Hebrews 4:14-16 shed light on this passage?

Look at the word righteous in verse 29. What does the phrase, "He is righteous" mean?

What do we who are born of Him do?

**Apply the Truth**: Do you feel shame before Jesus? Pray Romans 10:11 over your shame.

**Challenge**: Look up the Greek words for boldness and ashamed. What do they mean?

### Day 17: 1 John 3:1-3

**Read** this passage, at least twice, slowly. Out loud, if possible:

1 Look at how great a love the Father has given us that we should be called God's children. And we are! The reason the world does not know us is that it didn't know Him. 2 Dear friends, we are God's children now, and what we will be has not yet been revealed. We know that when He appears, we will be like Him because we will see Him as He is. 3 And everyone who has this hope in Him purifies himself just as He is pure.

What is our command in verse 1?

Let's do it! Write at least 3 ways you have known or experienced God's love for you:

Underline the word <u>know</u> every time it appears in today's passage.

What does the world not <u>know</u>? (verse 1)

What do we not <u>know</u>? (verse 2)

What can we <u>know</u>? (verse 2)

The words <u>purifies</u> and <u>pure</u> in verse 3 are taken from the same Greek word that means "proper, clean, innocent, modest, perfect, chaste."

According to this definition, how was Christ pure?

Understanding Christ's purity, what should we be doing? (verse 3)

**Apply the truth**: We will one day be "like Him" (verse 2); but for now, we strive to be pure "just as He is pure." In what areas of your life are you comfortably impure?

**Challenge**: Reflect on the many ways the phrase "how great a love" is written in other Bible translations.

### Day 18: 1 John 3:4-6

**Read** this passage, at least twice, slowly. Out loud, if possible:

4 Everyone who commits sin also breaks the law; sin is the breaking of law. 5 You know that He was revealed so that He might take away sins, and there is no sin in Him. 6 Everyone who remains in Him does not sin; everyone who sins has not seen Him or known Him.

Circle the word <u>sin</u> every time it appears in today's passage.

According to verse 4, what is <u>sin</u>?

How does Paul define <u>sin</u> in Romans 3:23?

What did Jesus teach about <u>sin</u> in John 8:34?

Who is <u>He</u> in verse 5?

Verse 6 seems contradictory to 1 John 1:8-10, which you studied in Day 4. Flip back and read that passage afresh.

The discrepancy comes in how we translate the verb <u>sin</u> in verse 6. The tense of the verb is not a one-time sin; it's a continuous, habitual action. The English Standard Version translates verse 6, "No one who abides in him keeps on sinning; no one who keeps on sinning has either seen him or known him."

How does Psalm 19:13 help us understand habitual sin?

What is the celebratory news revealed in verse 5?

**Apply the Truth**: Jesus was sinless and He alone gives you the power to overcome your habitual sin. Believe He can free you from your sin habits!

**Challenge**: Read Romans 3 and reflect on what sin is and how Jesus overcomes it.

### Day 19: 1 John 3:7-10a

**Read** this passage, at least twice, slowly. Out loud, if possible:

7 Little children, let no one deceive you! The one who does what is right is righteous, just as He is righteous. 8 The one who commits sin is of the Devil, for the Devil has sinned from the beginning. The Son of God was revealed for this purpose: to destroy the Devil's works. 9 Everyone who has been born of God does not sin, because His seed remains in him; he is not able to sin, because he has been born of God. 10 This is how God's children—and the Devil's children—are made evident.

John is delivering a hard truth in today's passage. Why might some Christians struggle to believe it?

John reveals his tender heart with the opening words, though: "Little children." He is speaking the truth in love (Ephesians 4:15), using a term of endearment followed by a strong warning.

The verbs in today's passage are the same tense as the verb <u>sin</u> from yesterday's passage, meaning "continually." Knowing that, finish the following statements:

(Verse 7) The one who continually does what is right...

(Verse 8) The one who continually sins...

What three characteristics do we learn about "everyone who has been born of God" (verse 9)?
1)

2)

3)

**Apply the Truth**: This passage cuts to the chase. Based on your continual actions, are you a Son of God or of the Devil?

**Challenge**: Observe the word "deceive" in Day 15 and today. What false teaching may deceive believers?

**Day 20: 1 John 3:10b-12**

**Read** this passage, at least twice, slowly. Out loud, if possible:

Whoever does not do what is right is not of God, especially the one who does not love his brother. 11 For this is the message you have heard from the beginning: We should love one another, 12 unlike Cain, who was of the evil one and murdered his brother. And why did he murder him? Because his works were evil, and his brother's were righteous.

Today's passage mentions Cain and his brother. Refresh your memory of their story by reading Genesis 4:1-16. Focus on Cain and his continual, habitual sin. Write your observations:

After spending several paragraphs describing the sinfulness of those who are not children of God, John is completing the thought he began at the beginning of chapter 3. Write a short summary of these verses:

1 John 3:1

1 John 3:2

1 John 3:11

Make a diagram that ties these three verses together:

Underline the word <u>especially</u> in verse 10. This word is pointing out the supreme example of not doing what is right. What is that, according to the last phrase of verse 10?

**Apply the Truth**: Be completely honest with yourself and God: Do you love others?

**Challenge**: How do John 13:34-35, John 15:17, and Romans 12:10 confirm today's passage?

**Day 21: 1 John 3:13-15**

**Read** this passage, at least twice, slowly. Out loud, if possible:


13 Do not be surprised, brothers, if the world hates you. 14 We

know that we have passed from death to life because we love

our brothers. The one who does not love remains in death. 15

Everyone who hates his brother is a murderer, and you know

that no murderer has eternal life residing in him.

According to verse 13, what should not surprise us?

Write what Jesus said about this very topic in John 15:18-19:


Circle the words <u>life</u> and <u>death</u> every time they appear in today's passage.

What proves we have passed from death to life? (verse 14)

What causes us to remain in death? (verse 14)


Now underline <u>hate</u> and <u>love</u> every time they appear in today's passage.

What do you learn about someone who <u>hates</u> in verse 15?


Look back at 1 John 2:25 (Day 14). How does that verse confirm what you learn in today's passage?


**Apply the Truth**: Who is it that you struggle to love? Another key to loving others is found in Matthew 22:37-39. What does it say?

**Challenge**: If verse 15 sounds familiar, it should. Jesus spoke similar words from the Sermon on the Mount (Matthew 5-7). Can you find them?

### Day 22: 1 John 3:16-17

**Read** this passage, at least twice, slowly. Out loud, if possible:

16 This is how we have come to know love: He laid down His life for us. We should also lay down our lives for our brothers. 17 If anyone has this world's goods and sees his brother in need but closes his eyes to his need—how can God's love reside in him?

(At this point in the study you might be thinking, "I feel like John keeps saying the same things over and over." YOU ARE RIGHT! He is focused on the most important things relating to faith and love and life! Don't tune him out!)

1 John 3:16 is similar to John 3:16.

Write John 3:16 here:

How does John 3:16 point to 1 John 3:16?

1 John 3:16 defines love but then gives us a command. What is it?

John heard these words come out of Peter's mouth in John 13:37-38. Summarize them:

What did Jesus teach about laying down your life in John 15:13?

1 John 3:17 gives the detail of how we lay down our lives. What is it?

**Apply the Truth**: Who do you know that is in need (verse 17) today? How can you show God's love by meeting that need?

**Challenge**: How do the words of John 10:14-18 help explain the meaning of 1 John 3:16?

**Day 23: 1 John 3:18-20**

**Read** this passage, at least twice, slowly. Out loud, if possible:

18 Little children, we must not love with word or speech, but with truth and action. 19 This is how we will know we belong to the truth and will convince our conscience in His presence, 20 even if our conscience condemns us, that God is greater than our conscience, and He knows all things.

Circle the word <u>must</u> in verse 18. Underline what we <u>must</u> do.

Briefly summarize what 1 John 3:16 said in yesterday's passage:

How did Jesus show His love in 1 John 3:16? Was it with "word or speech" or with "truth and action?"

Knowing that, why must we love with "truth and action?"

The word for <u>conscience</u> is the Greek word pronounced *kär-dē'-ä*, which is similar to our word <u>cardiac</u>. It means "heart, or the center of physical and spiritual life." It encompasses our "mind, passions, intelligence, will, character, and soul."

According to verse 19, what must we do to our conscience sometimes?

In verse 20, John teaches two things about God. What are they?
1)

2)

**Apply the Truth**: No matter what you think or believe or want, God's Truth prevails. Where do you clash with God's Word today?

**Challenge**: How do Jeremiah 17:9 and Psalm 51:10 teach us how to align our heart with God's Truth?

**Day 24: 1 John 3:21-24**

**Read** this passage, at least twice, slowly. Out loud, if possible:

21 Dear friends, if our conscience doesn't condemn us, we have

confidence before God 22 and can receive whatever we ask

from Him because we keep His commands and do what is

pleasing in His sight. 23 Now this is His command: that we

believe in the name of His Son Jesus Christ, and love one

another as He commanded us. 24 The one who keeps His

commands remains in Him, and He in him. And the way we

know that He remains in us is from the Spirit He has given us.

Review what you read about the word <u>conscience</u> yesterday.
Write it:

Today's passage reveals the importance of knowing the full
counsel of God's Word. What does verse 22 say about receiving
what we ask from God?


Now write what these passages say about receiving what we
ask from God:
1 John 5:14

John 16:24

James 4:3

In Jesus' model prayer in Matthew 6:9-13, whose desires are
sought?

According to verse 22, what must we do to receive what we
ask?

Verse 23 reveals what it means to "keep His commands" (verse
22). What is it?


According to verse 24, what happens when we keep His
commands?


Summarize how keeping God's commands affects our lives,
according to verses 22-24.


**Apply the Truth**: Which is more important to you: getting what
you ask or having the Spirit in you?

**Challenge**: How does Matthew 22:36-40 confirm today's
passage?

**Day 25: 1 John 4:1-3**

**Read** this passage, at least twice, slowly. Out loud, if possible:

1 Dear friends, do not believe every spirit, but test the spirits to determine if they are from God, because many false prophets have gone out into the world. 2 This is how you know the Spirit of God: Every spirit who confesses that Jesus Christ has come in the flesh is from God. 3 But every spirit who does not confess Jesus is not from God. This is the spirit of the antichrist; you have heard that he is coming, and he is already in the world now.

Underline the word spirit or Spirit every time it appears in today's passage.

The Greek word for *spirit*, pronounced *pnyü'*-mä, refers to the Holy Spirit when it is capitalized (as in verse 2). If not capitalized it refers to some other source of "power, affection, emotion, and desire. It is the disposition that fills and governs one's mind and will."

What do you learn about spirits in the world in verse 1?

What are we to do with the spirits? (verse 1)

How are we to "test the spirits," according to verses 2-3?

At the time John wrote this book, there was a false teaching that Jesus came as God in the form of man but that the heavenly part of Him left before the crucifixion.

We have a powerful weapon for testing every spirit. What does Ephesians 6:17 call "the sword of the Spirit?"

What "divides soul and spirit," according to Hebrews 4:12?

**Apply the Truth**: Only through God's Word can we truly know God's Spirit. Commit your mind and heart to knowing God's Word fully.

**Challenge**: Review what you learned about the antichrist on Day 11. Apply it to today's passage.

**Day 26: 1 John 4:4-6**

**Read** this passage, at least twice, slowly. Out loud, if possible:

4 You are from God, little children, and you have conquered them, because the One who is in you is greater than the one who is in the world. 5 They are from the world. Therefore what they say is from the world, and the world listens to them. 6 We are from God. Anyone who knows God listens to us; anyone who is not from God does not listen to us. From this we know the Spirit of truth and the spirit of deception.

In Scripture, always use your context to be sure you know who or what a pronoun replaces. (Grammar lesson: a pronoun takes the place of a noun.)

Underline the pronouns in this passage. (That includes they, them, we, us, and this.)

Beside each pronoun, write who or what the pronoun replaces. You will need to look back at yesterday's passage to determine who they and them are in verses 4-5.

Flip back to Day 10 to review what the word world means. Rewrite verse 5 using that definition in place of the word "world."

What phrase is repeated in verses 4 and 6?

Each repeated phrase reveals a promise. What are those two promises?
1)

2)

**Apply the Truth**: Write "I am from God" and "We are from God" as many times as you can today. Ask God to help you know and believe this truth.

**Challenge**: Write everything you can learn about the word spirit/Spirit from 1 John 4:1-6.

**Day 27: 1 John 4:7-11**

**Read** this passage, at least twice, slowly. Out loud, if possible:

7 Dear friends, let us love one another, because love is from

God, and everyone who loves has been born of God and knows

God. 8 The one who does not love does not know God, because

God is love. 9 God's love was revealed among us in this way:

God sent His One and Only Son into the world so that we might

live through Him. 10 Love consists in this: not that we loved

God, but that He loved us and sent His Son to be the

propitiation for our sins. 11 Dear friends, if God loved us in this

way, we also must love one another.

Circle the word <u>love</u> every time it appears in today's passage.

Love. Love. Love. Sometimes 1 John sounds like a broken record. And for good reason!

Where is love from? (verse 7)

What two things mark people who love? (verse 7)
1)

2)

How was God's love revealed? (verse 9)

Whose action defines love? (verse 10)

What did God do because of His love for us? (verse 10)

Knowing God's action defined love and sets the standard for love, what <u>must</u> we do? (verse 11)

Complete this summary using a form of the word "love" in each blank:
God is _____.
God _____ us.
We must _____ one another.

**Apply the Truth**: Read John 19, thanking Jesus for demonstrating the love of God.

**Challenge**: How many times can you find the phrase "Love one another" in 1 John?

**Day 28: 1 John 4:12-16**

**Read** this passage, at least twice, slowly. Out loud, if possible:

12 No one has ever seen God. If we love one another, God remains in us and His love is perfected in us. 13 This is how we know that we remain in Him and He in us: He has given assurance to us from His Spirit. 14 And we have seen and we testify that the Father has sent His Son as the world's Savior. 15 Whoever confesses that Jesus is the Son of God—God remains in him and he in God. 16 And we have come to know and to believe the love that God has for us. God is love, and the one who remains in love remains in God, and God remains in him.

Why hasn't anyone seen God? Read Exodus 33:18-23 and write God's explanation.

Verse 12 seems to jump from topic to topic: we can't see God; God's love is in us if we love one another. However, several translations (AMP, CEV, NIV, NLT, and others) insert the word But at the beginning of the second sentence of verse 12. How does the word "but" that enhance the meaning of the verse?

Verses 13-14 reveal the three distinct Persons of the trinity: Father, Son, and Spirit. In your own words, explain how the Three work together:

Verse 16 is worthy of your time and mental energy to memorize. Commit to reading it aloud several times a day in order to hide it in your heart. Why? It contains foundational truths!

**Apply the Truth**: Write verse 16 somewhere that you will remember to say it and meditate on it for the remainder of this study.

**Challenge**: How does the conversation between Peter and Jesus in John 6:66-69 reflect 1 John 4:16?

**Day 29: 1 John 4:17-19**

**Read** this passage, at least twice, slowly. Out loud, if possible:

17 In this, love is perfected with us so that we may have confidence in the day of judgment, for we are as He is in this world. 18 There is no fear in love; instead, perfect love drives out fear, because fear involves punishment. So the one who fears has not reached perfection in love. 19 We love because He first loved us.

Pronoun alert! Circle the word this in verse 17. What noun does this replace? (Look back at yesterday's scripture for the answer).

Sit heavy on this truth from verse 17:

"Love is _____ with us"

The Expanded Bible defines the word perfected like this: "made complete, comes to full expression."

How?
1) So that we may have _____ on the day of judgment. (verse 17)

2) When we have no _____ in love. (verse 18)

3) When we love because He _____. (verse 19)

Quick recap of 1 John 4:
God is love, God loves us, and He demonstrated His love by sending Jesus to die for our sins. But His love is made complete, or expressed fully, when we live in light of His love. When His love affects our confidence, our fear, and how we treat others.

**Apply the Truth**: Your faith and your love and your testimony are empty and void without love. Intentionally focus on how you can better love God and others.

**Challenge**: What does the phrase, "we are as He is in this world," (verse 17) mean?

**Day 30: 1 John 4:20-21**

**Read** this passage, at least twice, slowly. Out loud, if possible:

20 If anyone says, "I love God," yet hates his brother, he is a liar.

For the person who does not love his brother he has seen

cannot love the God he has not seen. 21 And we have this

command from Him: The one who loves God must also love his

brother.

Underline the word <u>love</u> every time it appears in today's passage. Circle the word <u>brother</u> every time it appears.

We close 1 John 4 today with a call to action. Rather, a call to analysis. This passage has three definite, plainly-stated truths:

1) If any one claims to love God and hates his brother, he is a _____.

2. The person who does not love his brother cannot _____.

3. We have this _____ from God: The one who loves God must also _____ his brother.

Summarize the above three truths in one sentence:

What did Jesus say about this topic in John 13:34?

What else did He say in Matthew 5:43-48?

What else did He say in Matthew 22:37-39?

What did James teach in James 2:14-17?

**Apply the Truth**: Personalize today's passage by inserting your name where appropriate.

**Challenge**: How does Galatians 5:13-15 bring today's truths to light?

**Day 31: 1 John 5:1-5**

**Read** this passage, at least twice, slowly. Out loud, if possible:

1 Everyone who believes that Jesus is the Messiah has been born of God, and everyone who loves the Father also loves the one born of Him. 2 This is how we know that we love God's children when we love God and obey His commands. 3 For this is what love for God is: to keep His commands. Now His commands are not a burden, 4 because whatever has been born of God conquers the world. This is the victory that has conquered the world: our faith. 5 And who is the one who conquers the world but the one who believes that Jesus is the Son of God?

We've entered the final chapter of John's passionate letter to believers. Not only is he wrapping up his thoughts but he is bringing out the main ideas one last time.

Underline or circle each of the words in today's passage that you have already seen several times in this book.

Today's passage is a great example of circular reasoning: starting with a truth and ending with the same truth. Fill in the blanks to see it come full circle:

Everyone who believes _____ has been _____. (verse 1)

Everyone who loves the father loves _____. (verse 1)

We love God's children when we _____ & _____. (verse 2)

_____ is the victory that has conquered the world. (verse 4)

The one who conquers the world believes _____.

LOVE IS DEFINED IN VERSE 3! What is it?

**Apply the Truth**: How is John's definition in verse 3 different from your own definition? How can you believe that John is telling you Truth?

**Challenge**: How do John 16:33, Romans 12:21, and Hebrews 11:33 expound on the truth of today's passage?

**Day 32: 1 John 5:6-8**

**Read** this passage, at least twice, slowly. Out loud, if possible:

6 Jesus Christ—He is the One who came by water and blood, not by water only, but by water and by blood. And the Spirit is the One who testifies, because the Spirit is the truth. 7 For there are three that testify: 8 the Spirit, the water, and the blood—and these three are in agreement.

Mark the words <u>water</u>, <u>blood</u>, and <u>Spirit</u> uniquely every time they appear in today's passage.

What does this passage teach you about <u>water</u> and <u>blood</u>?

What does this passage teach you about the <u>Spirit</u>?

Today's passage sounds much like a different passage, spoken by Jesus, in the gospel of John. What did He say about <u>water</u> and <u>Spirit</u> in John 3:1-8?

What do you learn about <u>water</u> and <u>blood</u> in Hebrews 9:19?

What is significant about <u>water</u> in Mark 1:10?

What does Jesus teach about <u>water</u> in John 4:14-15?

What do you learn about <u>water</u> and <u>blood</u> in Hebrews 10:19-22?

**Apply the Truth**: Meditate on the Biblical implications of these three words: water, blood, Spirit. Summarize what John is teaching.

**Challenge**: This is not a quickly understood passage! Seek wisdom from several sources or Bible experts.

**Day 33: 1 John 5:9-13**

**Read** this passage, at least twice, slowly. Out loud, if possible:

9 If we accept the testimony of men, God's testimony is greater, because it is God's testimony that He has given about His Son. 10 (The one who believes in the Son of God has this testimony within him. The one who does not believe God has made Him a liar, because he has not believed in the testimony God has given about His Son.) 11 And this is the testimony: God has given us eternal life, and this life is in His Son. 12 The one who has the Son has life. The one who doesn't have the Son of God does not have life. 13 I have written these things to you who believe in the name of the Son of God, so that you may know that you have eternal life.

Today we add a new key word from First John: <u>testimony</u>. Circle it every time it appears in today's passage.

The Greek word translated <u>testimony</u> in this passage is pronounced *mär-tü-rē'-ä*, which sounds a lot like our word "martyr." The basic definition of this word is "evidence."

Write "evidence" every time you circled the word "testimony." Re-read the passage, saying "evidence" in place of "testimony."

According to verse 9, what are the two types of testimony?
1)

2)

Which is greater? (verse 9)

What is God's testimony? (verse 11)


JESUS IS THE EVIDENCE OF GOD'S ETERNAL LIFE. He is proof that what God says about eternity is true. We don't need to wonder about our salvation; we can KNOW!


**Apply the Truth**: Personalize today's passage. Say it or write it with "I/me/my" instead of "you/one/we."

**Challenge**: What did Jesus do "so that (the audience) may know" in Matthew 9:1-7? How does this remind you of 1 John 5:13?

74

**Day 34: 1 John 5:14-15**

Read this passage, at least twice, slowly. Out loud, if possible:

14 Now this is the confidence we have before Him: Whenever we ask anything according to His will, He hears us. 15 And if we know that He hears whatever we ask, we know that we have what we have asked Him for.

Oh, what a glorious passage. What amazing promises!

What is the promise in verse 14?

What is the promise in verse 15?

Many people tend to skip over a phrase in this passage. Fill in the blank:

"Whenever we ask anything _____, He hears us." (verse 14).

Both the promises of this passage hinge on that truth. Write anything else you discover about asking <u>according to God's Will</u> in these passages:

Matthew 7:7-9


Matthew 21:22


John 14:13-14


John 15:7


John 16:24

**Apply the Truth**: How does your understanding of how to pray change your prayers?

**Challenge**: How did Jesus pray with this confidence in John 11:41-44?

**Day 35: 1 John 5:16-17**

**Read** this passage, at least twice, slowly. Out loud, if possible:

16 If anyone sees his brother committing a sin that does not

bring death, he should ask, and God will give life to him—to

those who commit sin that doesn't bring death. There is sin that

brings death. I am not saying he should pray about that. 17 All

unrighteousness is sin, and there is sin that does not bring

death.

Today's passage may bring concern or fear to your faith: "Just what is this sin that brings death? Have I done it?!?!"

One way to understand a passage you don't grasp is to look at other translations. Here is today's passage in The Voice translation, which will hopefully make it clearer:

16 In this regard, if you notice a brother or sister in faith making moral missteps and blunders, disregarding and disobeying God even to the point of God removing this one from the body by death, then pray for that person; and God will grant him life on this journey. But to be clear, there is a sin that is ultimately fatal and leads to death. I am not talking about praying for that fatal sin, 17 but I am talking about all those wrongs and sins that plague God's family that don't lead to death.

Underline the phrases above that help to clarify what you didn't understand the first time you read it.

Is the command to pray dealing with sins of believers or sins of unbelievers?

Combine the truths of today's passage with the truths of yesterday's passage. Together what are they teaching?

**Apply the Truth**: According to verse 17, what do our sins do to the family of God?

**Challenge**: How do Romans 6:23, 7:13, and 8:2 help you understand today's passage?

### Day 36: 1 John 5:18-19

**Read** this passage, at least twice, slowly. Out loud, if possible:

18 We know that everyone who has been born of God does not sin, but the One who is born of God keeps him, and the evil one does not touch him. 19 We know that we are of God, and the whole world is under the sway of the evil one.

Some translations use more capitals than others. This translation (HCSB) uses a capital letter for every reference to God, Jesus, and the Holy Spirit.

Find the word in today's passage that is capitalized to refer to a member of the trinity.

Who is that word talking about? (If you're not sure, find this passage in the Amplified, ESV, NCV, or NLV translation. You can find them all at biblegateway.com: type in 1 John 5:18, and click on "all English translations.")

The word translated keeps in verse 18 is the Greek word pronounced tā-re'-ō, which means "to guard, from loss or injury, properly, by keeping the eye upon."

Who is kept or guarded in verse 18? (Note the lower-case first letter!)

Who **does** the guarding in verse 18?

What happens when "the One who is born of God" is guarding us? (verse 18)


What confidence can we know, according to verse 19?

**Apply the Truth**: What makes you fearful? How does today's passage speak to your fears?

**Challenge**: Look up all English translations of verse 19. What do you learn about the difference in "we" and "the world?"

**Day 37: 1 John 5:20-21**

**Read** this passage, at least twice, slowly. Out loud, if possible:

20 And we know that the Son of God has come and has given us understanding so that we may know the true One. We are in the true One—that is, in His Son Jesus Christ. He is the true God and eternal life. 21 Little children, guard yourselves from idols.

Today's passage contains the end of John's letter. Verse 20 sounds like the perfect ending to a loving, passionate letter.

Underline the word <u>we</u> every time it appears in today's passage. Circle "Son of God" (and the pronoun <u>He</u> that replaces it) every time it appears.

What do you learn about the "Son of God"/"He" in verse 20?
1)

2)

3)

What do you learn about <u>we</u> in verse 20?
1)

2)

Verse 21 seems to come out of left field, as though John got to the end and realized he forgot a very important instruction. What is it?

What do you learn about idols in Psalm 115:4 and 135:14?

**Apply the Truth**: Your identity is found in this verse. Does your life reflect this truth?

**Challenge**: What else do you learn about guarding yourself from Deuteronomy 4:9 and Acts 20:28?

**Day 38: Review and Reflect**

You did it! You spent thirty-seven days digging deeply into the book of First John, taking in his words of truth and love and how to live.

Do you feel like a First John expert? Probably not. And that's good, because we are never done learning God's Word or even one portion of it. After all, the Bible is living and active (Hebrews 4:12)!

So don't check this book off your list. In fact, consider all the different ways you can continue to dig into First John:

**Summaries**
1) Go back through each day and write a one-sentence summary of each **day's** passage.

2) Based on your daily summaries, considered together, write a one-sentence summary of each **chapter**.

3) Based on your chapter summaries, write a one-sentence summary of the **book**.

**Key Words**
Some of the key words in the book of First John are as follows:
Know/knowledge
Love
Believe
Light/Darkness
Fellowship
Truth/Lie(s)
World
Remain/Abide
(There are more! Can you find them?)

1) **Identify** the Key Words by marking them in a distinct way. Use different colors or different kinds of underlining, circling,

boxing, or even a drawing (such as a heart on the word "love" every time it appears).

2) **Define** the key words if you haven't already. Use blueletterbible.org and click on the "Strong's" option, which gives you the original Greek words and their meanings.

3) **Make a list** of everything you learn about that word in the entire book. This will help you gather <u>all</u> the information and have a complete understanding of what John is teaching.

### The Trinity
1) Mark God/Jesus/Spirit uniquely throughout the book. (Don't forget to use the pronoun He that would also refer to each member of the trinity!)

2) Make a list of what you learn about God, Jesus, and the Holy Spirit based on everything John teaches.

### Us
1) Mark "we" and "you" uniquely each time they appear in the book.

2) Make a list of what John says about "we" and "you."

At every step, compare First John to other passages in Scripture. Pray over them. Find ways to internalize the truths by applying it to your life.

Keep knowing.
Keep believing.
Live!

Made in United States
North Haven, CT
30 March 2024

50703994R00048